YouTube Channel Success

Success

How To Create A Great YouTube Channel, Gain Millions Of Subscribers, And Make Money Too

BY

Ernie Braveboy

responsibility of the recipient reader. Under no circumstances will any legal responsibility or blame be held against the publisher for any reparation, damages, or monetary loss due to the information herein, either directly or indirectly.

Respective authors own all copyrights not held by the publisher.

The information herein is offered for informational purposes solely and is universal as so. The presentation of the information is without a contract or any type of guarantee assurance.

The trademarks that are used are without any consent, and the publication of the trademark is without permission or backing by the trademark owner. All trademarks and brands within this book are for clarifying purposes only and are the owned by the owners themselves, not affiliated with this document.

INTRODUCTION

I want to thank you and congratulate you for buying the book, "**YouTube Channel Success:** How To Create A Great YouTube Channel, Gain Million Of Subscribers, And Make Money Too."

Today, thanks to YouTube, anyone can be an influential media personality. YouTube is so potent a platform that other than the billions of people visiting the platform every day, it is also making many others millionaires.

Take the example of Daniel Middleton (DanTDM). His YouTube channel, a channel dedicated to video games, and that has over 19.8 million subscribers and well over 13.3 billion total video views, earns him upwards of $16.5 million annually, and he is not the only one. Evan Fong, Dude Perfect, PewDiePie, Smosh and Ryan ToysReview, and many other YouTubers generate millions of dollars off YouTube annually.

While we are not saying you will generate millions of dollars from YouTube, by creating an amazing YouTube channel populated with amazing content that people love to watch whether, for their education or entertainment, you can create a YouTube channel that has millions of subscribers and that generates passive income. This guide is going to show you among other things:

How to get started with YouTube (everything you need to know to get started),

1. How to grow your channel exponentially so that it has millions of followers,

2. How to increase traffic to your YouTube channel,

3. How to monetize your YouTube channel using the most effective monetization strategies as well as tons of other YouTube stuff that will get you ready for YouTube stardom:

Thanks again for buying this book. I hope you enjoy it!

TABLE OF CONTENTS

Section 1: Laying The Foundation

To create an amazing YouTube channel that attracts a loyal following, you need to lay a proper foundation because this foundation is the rock upon which you will build your YouTube Empire.

Most of the content in this section will be beginner geared in the sense that it will outline all the various elements you need to have in place to position your YouTube channel for maximum success.

Getting Started with YouTube:

Why YouTube?

If you are new to creating a YouTube channel, the first thing you are likely to ask yourself is, why YouTube? Why should you bother to create a YouTube channel or become a YouTube personality? Well, this short chapter is going to cover that by showing you some of the ways through which YouTube can enrich your life.

Video is the future

First off, as a society, we are gravitating more towards video content. Think about it. Whenever you visit your Facebook timeline, what are you likely to see more, video post-shares, or text posts? If your Facebook/social media timeline is like that of most people, you are likely to see more video posts/shares. This is because video content is the future. YouTube is the mother of all video platforms.

Whether you want to establish a social brand or any form of business, you will have to leverage the power of viral video marketing to grow your business. You should start a great YouTube channel because when you have one, you can easily share your amazing videos to your social media channels (thereby driving more traffic to the channel), and even easily embed the video content into your text/blog content.

Did you know that in any given month, 8 out of 10 people aged 18-49 watch YouTube videos? Did you also know that in any given hour, YouTube users upload more than 400 hours of video content?

What does this tell you? It should tell you that, no matter how you look at it, video content is the way to go. In fact, in the present environment, instead of starting a blog (you should still consider starting one); you should consider starting a YouTube channel and using it as your primary communication method with your chosen audience.

The power of video marketing

The power of video marketing is the other reason why you should consider starting a YouTube channel.

Because they are easy to absorb, videos, especially short and sweet ones that have a purpose—whether that purpose is entertainment or education—videos are easy to share on social media and other platforms. It is actually common for video shares to outdo text share, especially on social media.

When you create great videos, videos that your audience find valuable, they are likely to share the videos with their audiences who are then likely to share the video with their audiences or friend's list. The effect of this is that in the end, your 2-3 minutes video can go viral and within a short time.

What does this mean?

It means that if you create great videos, videos that look professional and that fulfill a need, you do not have to dedicate too much time to marketing: your videos will simply market themselves because users will want to share the value in them.

The money

We cannot fail to mention the money aspect. YouTube is an amazing way to generate passive income, an income that does not require your active time and energy input to continue trickling into your bank account.

Think of it this way.

YouTube is a content platform. Like a blog, once you publish a YouTube video, it is always available to all users interested in the topic covered by the video—to make sure users find your videos, you have to optimize your videos with keywords, something we shall talk about later. This means that if you create a viral video, a video that users want to view and share, and then monetize it, you can generate tons of dollars in passive income all without ever having to do anything other than uploading the video and engage in the initial marketing.

In the introductory part of this guide, we illustrated how thousands of YouTubers are leveraging YouTube to generate millions of dollars in revenue. These individuals are now so popular that their names are household brands in their chosen niche/industry.

If you create an amazing YouTube channel, you too can generate thousands if not millions of dollars in passive income each month. Before you can do that, however, you first need to choose your niche/topic of concentration. The next chapter talks about that.

THE RICHES ARE IN THE NICHES: WHY AND HOW TO CHOOSE A NICHE FOR YOUR YOUTUBE CHANNEL

A niche is a segment of a market or in this case, the topic of your YouTube channel. The reasons why you should choose a niche are as many as the sands of the ocean.

For the purpose of this guide, we shall restrict ourselves to very specific reasons that illuminate why, before you start creating your YouTube channel, you should dedicate a fair amount of time and thought to the topic of your channel.

Why Choosing A Niche Is So Important

First, as implied, a niche is a segment of a market or in simpler terms, we can define it as a smaller topic in a larger one. For instance, health is a general topic. Under it are smaller topics such as weight loss, the various diet plans, exercise, and many others. The same applies to many other topics: we have one main, umbrella topic under which we find many other smaller topics.

The title of this chapter reads something along "the riches are in the niche." No truer words exist. Part of the reason why the riches are in the niches has to do with targeting. When your approach to marketing is too broad—remember that to grow your YouTube channel to millions of views and subscribers, you will have to market it—your marketing strategy will have a weak bite and you will not get value for money. Think of it this way.

If you decide to target the general health and beauty category under which we find other categories such as tanning, cellulite treatment, facials, acne care, etc., your marketing strategy will be all over the place because you will be attempting to target different audiences that have different needs, desires, and wants.

On the other hand, if you choose to concentrate on acne care, for example, a niche or sub-category of the main category, your marketing plan is likely to be very effective because you will be endeavoring to fulfill the needs and desires of a targeted audience that want a specific outcome.

This simple explanation is why you should niche down. If you would like to learn a bit more about why the riches are in the niche—and covertly, why you should only start your YouTube channel after choosing a niche—you can read more at https://medium.com/multiplier-magazine/the-riches-are-in-the-niches-209dd235e3d8.

Now that you know that, let us discuss the process by which you can choose a niche for your YouTube channel:

Tips And Strategies For Choosing A Niche For Your YouTube Channel

You now know that without choosing your niche—and doing so diligently enough—you are likely to create a YouTube channel that sees minimal growth, views, and subscription (sometimes zero), and therefore, one that does not reward—by generating a passive income that can run into millions—all the hard work you do to create videos for YouTube.

When it comes to choosing a niche (for your YouTube channel, Blog, or whatever else—including business—), you should only have one thing in mind and that is to *choose a niche where you know you can provide immense value to a dedicated target audience.*

If you look at the most successful businesses (maintaining a YouTube channel is a lot like running a business—only a fun one—), you will note that most of them are successful because they offer their audiences immense value.

If you get into a niche where you do not provide value, you will fail to attract an audience, and, only by attracting an audience that loves your YouTube content can you grow what we can only call a successful YouTube business that has millions of subscribers and that pays you well.

To determine if you can give your target audiences the immense value they desire, you should follow but one rule: think of a topic that interests you—hobbies—or one that you would passionately like to learn more about. This can be anything; the galaxy, a new language, coding, web design, makeup, or whatever else you can imagine—and then determine if there are other people out there in the world that would love the content on the same topic.

An ideal niche is one where you create content, video or otherwise—in this case, video—on topics that excite you or you are passionate about and that have a ready audience. How do you determine if a niche has a ready audience?

You can do so in one of two ways. First, you can create a buyer persona, or you can use a Keyword research tool to determine how many people are using Google and other search engines to search for similar content. The two methods can work individually but work better when combined.

Here are the steps to follow to use both methods—individually and together—

Step 1: Create a list

Think of the topics you would like to create video content for YouTube on. As we said earlier, this can be anything; poetry, how to draw, how to learn X or Y, etc. Think of 10-50 topics. Do not worry, if you allow yourself a few minutes of quiet and creative thinking, you will come up with a healthy list of ideas.

Once you have your list, look it over and out of the ideas you have, circle 10 that inspire you the most, the ones that when you think of creating content on, ignite a spark of joy within you.

Buyer Persona

Now that you have your list of 10, think a little about the type of person that would be interested in the same type of online content. What is that person's age? Where is that person (in terms of geo-location)? What does that person do? What are his or her main interests and do they relate to your niche? What type of content is that person likely to absorb online?

In marketing, we call this creating a buyer persona. A buyer person helps you create a clear mental image of the type of persona that would be interested in the type of content you would like to create.

You can create a buyer persona online using tools such as Xtensio.

After creating a buyer persona for each of the 5 to 10 of your passion topics/niche, you now need to determine if that niche has a potential audience or simply put if the person you have described in your buyer persona is actually looking for relevant content on the niche.

Step 2: Research niche profitability

Niches/topics that have a low volume traffic quantity, which means that not that many people are looking for related content, will not perform well or help you generate millions of followers or a passive income.

To research the profitability of a niche, you can use a Keyword research tool. Start by asking yourself, "When this audience goes online, what type of content is he or she looking for?" Then using these metrics, come up with a list of at least 50 words that the person would type into his or her search box when looking for content on your intended topic.

An easy way to determine the type of content people are searching for on Google and other search engines are to head to your search bar and typing the same words in. For instance, if after looking over our list, we determine that we would like to create a YouTube channel dedicated to home cooking, we can postulate that the person typing such words into YouTube (YouTube runs on Google Search engine) is most likely looking for recipes.

If we head to YouTube and type a recipe, something like "pumpkin pie," these platforms will auto-populate the rest to show you what people are typing into the search bar:

YOUTUBE

pumpkin pie red
pumpkin pie recipe
pumpkin pie recipe from scratch
pumpkin pie recipe easy
pumpkin pie recipe with real pumpkin
pumpkin pie recipe minecraft
pumpkin pie recipe allrecipes
pumpkin pie recipe vegan
pumpkin pie recipe martha stewart

GOOGLE

best pumpkin pie

best pumpkin pie **recipe**
best pumpkin pie **in atlanta**
best pumpkin pie **from scratch**
best pumpkin pie **crust**
best pumpkin pie **cheesecake recipe**

From the above, we can see that creating a video on "how to create a pumpkin pie from scratch" means we shall have an audience because YouTube has shown us that people are typing those words into their search bars.

While this is great, on the back end, it may be that only 10 people (out of a world that has over 3.5 billion internet users) are typing those words into their search bars; enter a keyword research tool.

A keyword research is a tool used by online marketers to determine how many people are typing specific words into their search engine bars. The more people typing specific keywords into their search engines, the more likely you are to have a potentially profitable niche.

To determine how many users are typing specific keywords into their search boxes—we4 call this average monthly searches or AMS can use a free keyword research tool such as Google Keyword Planner or a paid one such as AHREF.

For instance, when we type pumpkin pie into Google keyword planner, we can see the following results from which we can see that the terms "easy pumpkin pie recipe" have 1,000 to 10,000 monthly searches. This means that 1-10k people are typing these exact keywords into their search boxes, which means that, if we create a video on the same, assuming we do a great job of creating amazing content and optimizing it for search engines, we can get over 10,000 views on our "easy pumpkin pie recipe" YouTube video.

Keyword (by relevance)	Avg. monthly searches [?]	Competition [?]	Suggested bid [?]	Ad impr. sh:	Add to plan
easy pumpkin pie recipe	1K – 10K	Low	$1.84		»
easy pumpkin pie	1K – 10K	Low	$0.67		»
pumpkin pie recipe easy	1K – 10K	Low	$0.76		»
easy recipe for pumpkin pie	100 – 1K	Medium	$0.78		»
pumpkin pie easy recipe	100 – 1K	Low	$1.80		»
recipe for easy pumpkin pie	10 – 100	Low	$0.62		»

The goal of keyword research is to help you pursue a niche that has a potential high traffic volume. Choose to go into your preferred niche only if it has an average monthly search of 1-10k; choosing a niche whose main topics see 10-100 monthly searches is why most people create YouTube channels that flop and fail to take off.

Take your list of possible niches through this process and use the information you gather to choose a niche that fills you with passion and whose content on the same has a ready target audience.

In some instances, after taking your list of possible niches through this process, you may determine that your intended niche, the one that fills you with the most creative passion—remember that creating viral videos for YouTube requires tons of creativity—lacks a high search volume.

If that is the case, think of your main goal: what do you want your YouTube video content to achieve? Once you have this, simply think of the type of person that would want to view or that content. The buyer person you create from this will greatly help you determine which words such a person is likely to type when searching for content on YouTube or Google.

You can learn more about choosing a niche for your YouTube channel from https://medium.com/@diana_21435/how-to-choose-the-best-niche-for-your-youtube-channel-2e0fb5f465b0

This https://toughnickel.com/self-employment/10-Most-Profitable-YouTube-Niche-Ideas outlines a list of the 10 most popular YouTube niches (you can use it for inspiration)

Now that you have one or two topics that have proven to have a healthy traffic potential (and align with your passions), the next part is to create your YouTube channel and start populating it with valuable content that will thrill your audiences.

The next chapter talks in brief about how to set up your YouTube channel fast.

Setting Up: Creating Your YouTube Channel Fast

As suggested by the title of the chapter, this chapter seeks to help you create your YouTube channel as fast as possible. When we say set up, what we are actually talking about is creating the backbone of your channel in a way that sets you up for massive success.

Let us get started:

Setting up your YouTube channel is an easy feat. All you have to do is sign up for one using your Google account (Gmail account really). You can even use the same Google mail (Gmail) address to register multiple YouTube channels, which should prove very effective.

After creating your Google account (if you don't have one; if you do, all you have to do is sign in), Head over to YouTube—the homepage, which you can find on the link below—and from there, navigate to your account, which should be a thumbnail of your picture on the top right corner of your browser page.

Doing this will call up a drop-down menu; from there, you can choose to go to your Creator Studio, which is essentially the backend of your YouTube channel or create one if you have not. Clicking the creator studio should bring you to the following page:

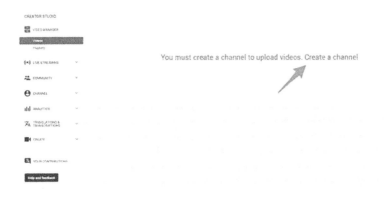

From there, the process of creating a YouTube channel is very straightforward and easy. To ensure that you go through this process in a way that prepares your channel for massive success, you ought to pay attention to specific elements the most important of which we shall now discuss:

Important Elements To Pay Attention To When Creating Your Successful YouTube Brand

The first and perhaps the most important thing you should pay special attention to is the name. Your YouTube name is your first audience contact point. Make sure the name is representative of your YouTube channel brand; make it memorable.

You can choose a YouTube channel name based on your niche, i.e. if you are in the makeup niche, you can name your channel based on this, or you can come up with a creative, memorable name.

Take the example of PewDiePie (read Pie-Die-Pie), a channel primarily in the gaming niche. The proprietor of the channel, Felix Arvid Ulf Kjellberg, says the name is creative the 'pew' in the name is the sound made by laser guns in video games while the "die" part means what happens after someone fires a laser gun: death (in the video game).

A great YouTube name will make it easier to brand your YouTube enterprise.

The other thing you want to pay attention to is the style. Here, you will want to concentrate on your overall outlay, your channel art including channel image and profile picture, how you organize your content, your channel description, and channel trailer (a video that plays automatically every time someone lands on your channel's homepage).

https://blog.bufferapp.com/create-a-youtube-channel resource has great content on the various elements you need to optimize as well as change (it also shows you exactly how to make those changes).

Once you have optimized the various elements of your new channel, you can then start creating and uploading videos. The next chapter talks about the various tools and equipment you need to shoot amazing video.

NOTE: As you start uploading video, you will note that, initially, YouTube will restrict your content length to less than 15 minutes. To remove this restriction, you need to verify your account as fast as possible so that Google bots can start viewing you as a real person instead of a bot that just creates accounts.

The verification process is easy; once you get to the verification page, all you will need to do is verify your account by inputting into the dialog box the code Google sends to your mobile phone.

YOUR ESSENTIAL YOUTUBE CREATOR EQUIPMENT GUIDE

The amazing thing about being a great YouTube content creator is that, once you have a great topic that inspires you and that has an audience ready to appreciate the value your video content ads to their life—whether that is education (video tutorials) or fun (funny video compilations)—you do not need much to start. Actually, the camera on your smartphone is enough to get you started.

However, since the idea is to create great video content—creating great, valuable content is how you create a successful YouTube channel—you need to go above your smartphone camera: start there yes, but evolve fast.

The following are the bare minimum (the essential) equipment you need to start out fast.

1: Camera

Depending on the nature of your video channel, you can start with a quality webcam. If you have a bit more, you can buy a quality DSLR camera. Only buy a high-end camera after YouTubing for a while (6-12 months is ideal) and verifying that your niche has a ready audience and the potential to grow into a full-time business.

When considering which camera to use, remember that the quality of your videos will also determine its popularity. Do not go for a camera that does not shoot anything below 720P.

2: Tripod

If your camera lacks a tripod, you will need one so that you can shoot steady videos. A tripod will offer you immense flexibility even when you are shooting on your mobile phone (we have tripods for mobile phones).

Nevertheless, tripods are not exactly essential because if you are shooting still video, you can place your camera atop books or other household items—many YouTubers do this.

3: Microphone

If you are in the tutorial or explainer niche, you will need a quality microphone since most of the available cameras—whether DSLR or your iPhone or smartphone—lack a robust microphone.

Get yourself an external microphone that has great sound quality and separates audio recording capabilities so that you can record audios separately and then mix it into the video afterwards for amazing sound.

Microphones can be expensive. Evaluate your microphone needs depending on the type of content you intend to create and move from there.

4: Green screen

A green screen is not essential; still, it comes in very handy when you want a clear background or to add effects to your recording environment. You can DIY a green screen using a sheet and some green dye, or you can buy one for $50 or less.

5: Video capture and audio editing tools

If you will be uploading content captured from your screen, which can be video tutorials, you will need a capable screen capture software. You have plenty of choices; you can use OBS studio, Snagit, CamStudio, or any other capable video capture software.

You will also need to have video editing software of which you have many options depending on your operating system. Before you splurge on expensive video and audio editing software, remember that the creator studio has an in-built video editing suite.

Good video editing software will also have capable audio editing tools to you can use; if that is not the case, or you have recorded your audio separately, you will need a quality audio editor so that you can clean your audio before you mix it with the video.

As your channel grows and generates a passive income, you can then splurge and build a real recording studio for your YouTube business. You can build a low-cost recording studio dedicated to growing your channel. https://www.makeuseof.com/tag/build-low-cost-youtube-studio/ resource talks about what you need to do that (mind you, you should only do this after your channel has grown to a specific point).

At this point in the guide, you should be ready to create great content for your YouTube channel. You should be ready to grow it too. Experiment with your new equipment and shooting a few video content for your channel. Edit and upload the videos as you get your feet wet with using the creator studio.

Now that you have chosen a niche, researched it, and then created great content for your waiting audience, content that adds value to their lives, you are ready to grow your

YouTube channel into a thriving brand/business. The chapters in the next section talk about this at length.

Section 2: Growing Your Channel - How To Create A Great YouTube Channel & Gain Millions Of Subscribers

Now that you have laid the foundation upon which your YouTube channel will thrive, you are ready to take it to the next level. At this point, you should be in a position where you are creating videos consistently and can comfortably use the various equipment and tools at your disposal.

How to Create a Great YouTube Channel that Has a Rabid Following and Million of Subscribers

First, to create a great YouTube channel, you should make sure you are in a niche that has the traffic potential so that when you create great video content and then optimize this content for search, you can drive organic traffic to your YouTube videos and channel.

Before we look at the ingredients, you need to create a standout YouTube channel that has a viral following and that earns you money, let us talk about video quality and how it affects your channel's success.

How To Create Videos That Attract Viral Views

YouTube is a search engine. Therefore, to create great content—content is what drives a channel to stardom—you will need to optimize your content and channel in the same way you would optimize a blog.

Once you start creating videos, you will want to improve your video quality as fast as possible because to get more views—more views often lead to a higher subscription—you will need to create quality content and then optimize it for search. We shall shortly discuss how to optimize your video content for search.

If you concentrate on the following three elements/steps, you should create quality video content that attracts viewership and helps you create a loyal following.

1: The purpose of the video

The purpose of the video—what it intends to do; either entertain or educate/accomplish—is at the very heart of how to create great YouTube channel that has quality content and thus, an amazing viewership.

When creating your YouTube content, always keep in mind that the people who will view it will have two main outcomes in mind: entertainment or education. For instance, someone looking for content on how to apply makeup is looking to solve a problem. Make sure that your content accomplishes both or at least one (educational videos with a funny twist or an element of personality are especially popular).

Understating that YouTube viewers (and all online users for that matter) are looking to fulfill these two needs will greatly influence the type of content you create. Aim to create videos that help your users solve their problem or accomplish what they want as first as possible.

This means that, while your videos should have a catchy introduction—perhaps a channel's theme song—you should not drag it out or the problem. Produce to-the-point video content; only by doing so, will see you attract and grow a loyal following as well as YouTube video views.

2: Quality trumps quantity

Common advice is to upload regularly. This is great advice and indeed, frequently uploading new video content is one of the key YouTube success factors.

Nevertheless, always remember that a channel producing and uploading 100, low-quality content per month cannot outmatch one that produces and uploads even 20, extremely high-quality content. This is in line with best SEO practices.

When we talk of quality content, we mean quality in terms of the video content—if it helps the viewers achieve their desired outcome—and quality in terms of how you shoot the videos. To create a great channel, you need to remember that low-quality videos are not how you get there.

A high-quality video is one that looks professionally shot— whether you are shooting from your webcam, YouTube studio or wherever else does not matter, the video has to be of high quality. This kind of video is clear, well lit, and not blurry. It oozes professionalism and s as if someone has truly invested in its quality.

To create such a video, you can use the classic white or green background. Such a background makes your video content look crisp and professional; it keeps the audiences' view focused on you instead of the things in your background. This type of setup is especially ideal for instances where you are shooting presentations of yourself (in-front-of-the-camera shoots).

Depending on your niche and the type of content you create, you can also use a whiteboard video where you narrate video drawings on a whiteboard. Whiteboards are especially great when you are creating explainer videos.

Unlike white background videos that are relatively easy to shoot—you simply need a white background and a nice enough camera placed on a tripod (a good microphone is also essential—whiteboard videos require special illustration skills. If you lack these skills, you can hire a freelancer.

High-quality videos also feature great editing, which is why video editing software made it to the list of things you will need to set up a successful YouTube business. If you do not know how to edit your videos, you can hire someone. Nevertheless, we will briefly discuss how to edit your YouTube video content.

3: Brandable

Being a YouTube creator is a lot like—at least to some degree—owning a TV show, which is why for a channel to be successful, it needs regular viewership. To create an Amazing video show, you need to make a name for yourself and your YouTube channel. The best way to do this is by uploading video content regularly.

Commit yourself to create, editing, and uploading new video content with some predictable frequency. Make sure that your channel has a great video offering. As you get started, upload new content frequently; doing so will give your channel more SEO juice on YouTube.

Having more videos is also a great chance to attract a healthy viewership as well as grow your subscriber list because even if someone does not like one of your first videos, another video offers you a chance to impress that audience and turn him or her into a subscriber.

As you grow your YouTube channel—, which, inadvertently, grows as you upload more, high-quality videos—your viewership and subscriber list will grow. This growth is not linear. The growth is likely to start low where your videos get minimal views and your subscribers list is as empty as an empty cobbler's curse. Gradually, however, the growth will be exponential especially if you have done a great job at niche selection and producing shareable content.

Because optimizing your YouTube content for search is the best way to increase your YouTube following and grow your YouTube channel (views, subscribers, and even revenue), you must ace this prospect of your YouTube empire. The next chapter of this section shows you how to do just that.

YOUTUBE GROWTH HACKING: OPTIMIZING YOUTUBE CONTENT FOR SEARCH AND IMPROVED VIEWS AND SUBSCRIBERS

Ensuring that your YouTube content generates as many quality views as possible is what turns a YouTube channel into a success. To ensure that your videos are generating views consistently and that your viewers are watching a large portion of your video content, you have to create great videos, which we have already covered how to do, and then optimize this content for search so that your videos appear as the most relevant for your intended keywords.

The general rule of growth hacking your YouTube channel's success is to ensure that your videos generate at least 3,600 views soon after uploading them. To a search engine such as YouTube, the difference between 0 and 2,000 is larger than the difference between 2,000 and 200,000, which means once you clock a few thousand views (over 3,000 views to be precise), you can easily rank first for your intended keywords assuming you optimize all the other SEO factors such as rating and user retention.

Aim to drive at least several thousand views to each video as soon as you upload it; this will ensure your channel rolls on forwarding full steam. How do you get these views as fast as possible? That depends on the nature of your niche and audience. Some effective optimization strategies include:

Cross Promotion

In cross-promotion, you leverage an already existing fan base. This method works best when you have a following—no matter how small—within your chosen niche. Another way to cross promote your channel is to ask other top YouTubers in your niche to host you (you participate in their video) so that you can gain access to their audience; obviously, this prospect works best when you have chosen a valuable contributor within your niche.

At the end of the cross-promotion video, have a call to action asking users of that channel to subscribe to your channel and ensure you have a keyword optimized (specifically optimized for the subject covered by that specific video) link to your channel on the video's description text.

How do you find channels on which you can cross promote? The easiest way to do this is to type your intended keywords—the ones you want to rank for—on YouTube and from the results, monitor the number of views and subscribers a channel has; the higher the subscriber list, the better for you.

After you find several such targets, simply email them with an offer to create valuable video content for their channel (always remember that as long as you provide value to an existing target audience, your YouTube channel will be a success).

Email Marketing

Again, if you have already established yourself as an authority in your niche, perhaps through a blog or social media, you should promote your content to that audience preferably via email—assuming you have in place an effective email collection strategy.

As stated earlier, while you can create YouTube as a standalone business, you are better of coupling it with a blog that allows you to create and post an accompanying blog post for each video you upload. You can then embed the corresponding YouTube video into the blog post for improved SEO juice to your blog as well as YouTube video and channel.

A blog as an accompaniment to your YouTube business is a great way to ensure that you give readers more options. Some will opt to read the blog while others will opt to view the video. In all though, a blog will present you a rare opportunity. It will allow you to entice your audience with a great free offer in exchange for their email addresses, which is only great for your YouTube channel since it means that every time you create new content, you can market to your list to drive tons of views to your videos.

Still, on email marketing, another effective way to drum up more views and subscribers—not to mention optimize your content for search—is to embark on an email outreach campaign. An email outreach campaign simply means creating a list of top bloggers, YouTubers, and Vloggers in your niche, and then asking them to share your high quality, extremely valuable content with their audiences. If you provide immense value to your target audience—and theirs since you are in similar niches—these individuals will be more than likely to oblige you.

As your YouTube channel grows and your views rack up, the subscriber list will grow on automatic as you retain your target through valuable video content. At this point, you can then consider using other promotion strategies such as paid advertising on Google and other platforms such as social media where you use paid advertising to expose your content to a larger audience base.

If you do this, your channel will generate tons of views and subscribers. Once you have this structure in place, you can then move to optimize your channel for search and thereby, improved growth (growth is how you build a YouTube channel that has millions of views and subscribers). Let us talk about the various elements you should optimize.

YouTube SEO Hacks: The Important Elements To Optimize

First, you should understand that the quality of your video matters the most. Trying to optimize a bad video is a futile effort. The elements that make a video of high quality are great recording (high-quality video and sound, lighting, etc.), and high-quality content that helps users solve a problem or fulfill a need.

Always remember that at the heart of YouTube success lies in one secret: provide so much value that your target audience has no choice but to take note. Make sure your message—and the mediums you use to communicate it—resonate with your target base.

Once you have that in place, optimize the following elements

NOTE: To optimize your YouTube video content, you will need to perform keyword research. Keywords are an integral part of ranking your YouTube videos first since the YouTube search engine is very similar to Google. The better and more targeted your keywords are, the higher your chances of ranking first, and the more likely you are to grow your channel fast.

For keyword research, you can use a free or paid keyword research tool. You can learn more about keyword research for YouTube https://backlinko.com/hub/youtube/youtube-keyword-research and https://longtailpro.com/keyword-research-for-youtube/.

Once you have your list of keywords, you will want to optimize:

Title

Your intended keywords should appear significantly on your title; this increases visibility and ensures that when users type those exact keywords into YouTube, the search engine matches their search query to your content as the most relevant.

Essentially, ensuring your keywords are in the title of your video means you should dedicate a substantial amount of thought and time to coming up with unique video headlines. The rule of thumb is to make the titles appealing to humans while at the same time making the titles search engines friendly by integrating your keywords into the title.

Meta

Ensure your videos have a human-oriented description that is also keyword rich. Nevertheless, keep in mind that the idea of a Meta description is to help audiences know the nature of the video and therefore, your use of keywords within the Meta description should not compromise this ability. Create keyword optimized Meta descriptions that stir up interest and click through in your audience.

Because the description will appear against each search results, make the description brief, to the point, and where possible without compromising human readability, keyword rich.

Tags

While not compulsory, tags help YouTube associate your video content with text, which means that can greatly improve your video ranking. Use keyword-optimized tags but avoid overdoing it by using irrelevant tags or too many tags.

Video thumbnail

Successful YouTube channels are ones that aim to create a brand by creating a sort of baseline element of their business. On YouTube, the best way to do this, to create a sort of uniformity and therefore, a visually pleasant

YouTube channel that is both memorable and enticing to its intended target audience, great, visually pleasing, and optimized-for-your-niche video thumbnails are the best way to do this.

Great thumbnails will give your channel a great aesthetic you want and help you create a brand around your chosen niche. The following screenshot shows the power of video thumbnails on YouTube as a branding and effective marketing tool:

Stand For Something In Your
Content and Leaning On

308 views · 2 months ago

Structuring Video In Your
Business Does Not Fall On

395 views · 4 months ago

How 7-Figure Entrepreneurs
Are Using Video In Their

371 views · 4 months ago

VLOGS   PLAY ALL

Making a 3 Part Video Series
For a Product Launch -

Sold With Video
1.2K views · 2 years ago

Why Do I VLOG on a Video
Marketing Channel? - VLOG

Sold With Video
580 views · 2 years ago

How To Make a Brick Wall
Video Set (DIY) - VLOG #12

Sold With Video
1.8K views · 2 years ago

Image courtesy of Sold With Video, a great YouTube channel that offers great tutorials on how to market your videos.

The channel has over 34k subscribers (34,127 subscribers to be exact), and most of its video uploads have an average of 1.2k views with some attracting as much as 450k views. That means that, on one specific video, 450,000 people are viewing and actively engaging with his content.

This proves that the channel and the topic it covers has a great viewership that the proprietor of the channel can capitalize on by providing immense value within the niche and then finding easy ways to monetize the channel.

To create thumbnails and therefore a brand around your video content, you can use https://support.google.com/youtube/answer/72431?hl=en resource from Google or watch a video on how to do so https://www.youtube.com/watch?v=Uby_wyOoBQ4.

For great video thumbnails, make the image as large and as light as possible. YouTube recommends that you *"keep your image **1280x720** and upload in image formats such as as.JPG, GIF, BMP, or.PNG."*

You can watch https://www.youtube.com/watch?v=VyToVPBU9Do great video tutorial on how to edit your image easily using free tools.

Closed Captions

YouTube is a video-based search engine. Like Google (the search engine), it depends on information (such as your video titles and their relevance to your niche, name of your channel, the links pointing back to your videos, user interaction with videos, and other metrics), to determine which search results are most relevant to user queries.

When you add closed captions and subtitles to your video content, you give the search ranking bots at Google more signals to relate the nature of your content to its users. Subtitles and CC (closed captions) are also a great way to allow users to interact with your content even when they are in noisy (or even quiet) environments.

Google has a great tutorial on how to add CC and subtitles to your video content:

If you prefer immersive learning (video learning), watch this amazing video by Roberto Blake, a creative entrepreneur whose YouTube channel has a subscriber list of 335k:

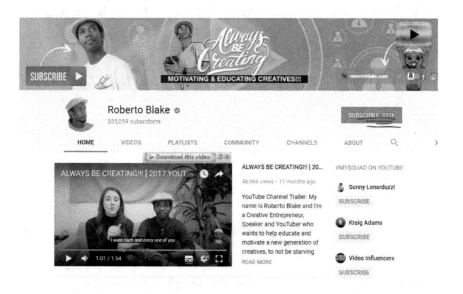

To ensure you are also creating a tribe around your content (doing this is how you become a leader in your industry by proving yourself a valuable contributor within that niche), you make your content—and channel—as interactive as possible.

You can improve your ranking, video views, and even subscription by encouraging your target audience to interact with your Video content, which improves engagement, and by giving you feedback on the value you are offering; interaction with your audience can help you come up with great content ideas.

Improving engagement and interaction is an especially important ranking factor that Google uses to determine the quality and relevance of video content so that it can give its users the best and most relevant search results. The amount of time a YouTube user watches your video is especially important. To improve this, use the first 15 seconds of your video to capture your audience's attention and then build great content from there.

Once you create great content that attracts a viewership, you can then concentrate on building your subscriber list. In most cases, your subscriber's list will start out slow but gain great momentum as you create great engaging content for a ready audience.

Add a Call to Action (CaT) to all your videos as a way to remind your audiences that if they liked the content and found it useful, they should like, comment on, and share your content, and subscribe to your channel for tons of other valuable content on your niche of concentration.

You can see why that'd be effective.

https://youtu.be/LOI_zSR-BPo has a great tutorial on how to overlay a call to action into your videos.

You can also drive up your engagement using an End-screen, the content that plays 5-20 seconds before the end of a video. You can use this segment to promote engagement on your channel (engagement in terms of views, comments, shares across different channels, and even your subscriber list).

https://www.youtube.com/watch?v=GlQEU-LCiVo video resource will show you how to add an end screen to your videos. If you are great at video editing, you can also edit your video to add an end screen using your preferred video editing suite or software.

Now that you have set up your channel for success and are creating great content (and uploading it regularly) so that you can drive up your rapidly growing audience, you should start to consider monetizing your channel, which we shall talk about in within the chapters of the next section.

For the moment though, it is important to mention that how potent an income strategy YouTube turns out to be for you will greatly rely on your ability to provide value in a niche market. How you do this, which will greatly determine how you approach the endeavor, will depend on your niche and what you want your channel to accomplish in the end.

As long as you are providing value, your channel will grow and continue to grow to a point where your audiences consider you an authority and are willing to pay you to consume more of your content, and where sponsors approach you for collaboration on interesting projects that pay you well because they want access to your audience.

You can start monetizing your content from the first video (even before you create tons of content) or start monetizing after you have created several videos and a growing audience. The great thing is that as you learn more about YouTube marketing and creating a shareable and interactive YouTube channel, your ability to grow your channel in every way possible—including engagement, views, subscribers, and monetization—will also improve.

To learn more about growing your YouTube channel the right way, you can read the content on https://www.socialmediaexaminer.com/15-tips-growing-youtube-channel/ resource. While we have adeptly covered most of these YouTube growth hacks, Jeremy West, A YouTube certified, top, YouTube-for-business expert whose channel and various videos have attracted over a billion views, has some gems and a great perspective on the topic

YouTube should only be one part of your monetization strategy. YouTube is usually at the top end of a marketing funnel—since YouTube is a tool used to gain the attention of potential audiences.

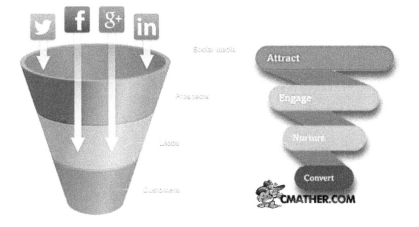

To monetize your channel, drive your YouTube followers to specific pages on your website (or even YouTube videos) where you can then ask them to take an action. The action can be to an offer intended to capture their email, or a sale pitch to promote a product you feel would help them achieve their desired end—which can be a landing page or video that sells something the audience wants.

This is the simplest trick to monetizing a YouTube channel the right and simple way. Remember that your ability to monetize your channel will largely depend on your niche, the value you create within it, and how you go about ensuring that your target audience sees this value and interacts with it.

Once you can do this, you can monetize using various avenues as discussed in the next section.

SECTION 3: YOUTUBE MONETIZATION - HOW TO IMPLEMENT THE MOST EFFECTIVE YOUTUBE MONETIZATION STRATEGIES

How you monetize your channel—including how long it takes your channel to start running itself and paying you (in terms of revenue generated)—will depend on your approach.

If you approach YouTube marketing as you would a business—one driven by your passions notwithstanding—you will put time and effort to creating a great YouTube channel that uploads great content consistently and whose content users consider valuable in whichever sense. Because of this, your audience will grow fast (and continue growing) so that in the end, you can monetize fast and grow your revenues even faster.

If, on the other hand, you approach it as a hobby, your effort to monetize your YouTube channel or grow your views, shares, and subscribes, will take longer since you will not be actively interacting with your intended targets regularly.

If you learn nothing else from this section, let what you learn to be that *"To create a great YouTube channel that generates revenue, you have to provide immense value consistently and in whichever format or way most appealing to your target audiences."*

If you do this, your channel will grow fast and start generating revenue even faster; how much revenue will depend on individual niches as well as how you monetize your YouTube channel since there are many ways to do so.

YouTube Monetization Strategies: How To Monetize Your YouTube Channel For Recurring Passive Income

We have various ways through which you can turn your amazing YouTube channel into a revenue-generating machine. This chapter discusses the most effective of these strategies and outlines how you can infuse them into your marketing strategy.

YouTube Partner Program (YPP): The Easiest Way to Monetize a Successful YouTube Channel

Since you have a keen interest in creating a successful YouTube channel that pays you and for its upkeep, you know that the easiest way to monetize your YouTube content is to serve ads on your content. This simply means allowing Google to serve your audience, relevant, audience-based ads, ads paid for by advertisers—revenue that Google shares with you, which is how you generate revenue.

The online space has tons of content on how to add Google adverts to your content. You can read more https://support.google.com/youtube/troubleshooter/7367 438?hl=en#ts=7367346.

After having a difficult year in 2017—difficulty in terms of advertisers' backlash because of the metrics Google uses to serve specific videos on specific channels—Google has chosen to change their metrics to ensure that the adverts served on videos and channels are in line with brand marketing and that ads run on relevant content. They now have a stricter policy for those looking to monetize using ads

Previously, to monetize your channel, you needed a minimum of 10,000 cumulative views (on all your videos) to gain eligibility to the partner program (YPP):

Google has been using this to determine which channels can run adds. Since Google considers letting you run ads a privilege, they have stopped basing their acceptance into the partner program on mere views.

Today, they take into account audience engagement, channel size, the frequency of upload, social shares, and various other factors to determine which channels they give the right to run ads. Google now only gives the ability to run ads to channels that have a subscriber list larger than 1,000 and 4,000 hours of content uploaded within the last 12 months.

Size is not the only metric they use. In their bid to determine a channel's compatibility with their partner program, they also use other signals such as spam, likes, community strikes, and abuse flags.

Their need to implement these "hard-to-game user signals" is in line with their purpose: to serve users the most relevant, high-quality content and at the same time reward YouTube creators (that means you) who are helping them provide their users with engaging content that helps them fulfill their needs.

Google is also changing their metrics for Google Preferred with the intent being to ensure that the platform serves the most popular and highly valuable content on YouTube using vetting measurements such as engagement, views, channel subscribers, and other metrics such a social shares and SEOP optimization.

With that said, as long as you are providing immense value to your constantly growing audience, YouTube Partner Program is the simplest way to monetize your YouTube channels since, as long as your channel meets their guidelines and thresholds, Google will give you access to the program and you can start using it to monetize your channel.

The great thing about the platform is that it allows you great flexibility in determining where the ads appear.

YPP Ads for monetization: key takeaways and the money potential

How much you stand to earn from running ads on your YouTube video depends largely on your daily video views and engagement.

You can use the calculator https://influencermarketinghub.com/youtube-money-calculator/ to determine your potential earnings. With that in mind, however, remember that your daily views and engagement will determine four other factors that are central to how much you actually end up earning through YouTube partnership program.

The *"cost per click"* (CPC), how much Google pays you for users who click on the ad or watch an ad, will determine your conversion rate. Your *"estimated gross income for every 1,000 views,"* which is how much Google pays out for an average 1,000 ad views for channels within your niche. Your *"estimated earnings per subscriber"* will also factor in, and so will your *"estimated variance based on video engagement."*

Growing you channel expeditiously is the best way to earn more income because the more people you have viewing your content and engaging with it—commenting, sharing, etc.—the higher the number of people seeing and clicking the ads Google serves on your channel and videos, and the higher your revenue earning potential.

Uniting your successful YouTube channel for the Google partner program is the best and easiest way to monetize your YouTube channel. With that said, how much income you actually generate from servings ads this way will be dismal ($100 or less per month), which may not be enough to sustain your channel and your ability to create better valuable content. Hence, you should constantly work to diversify your earnings using other avenues.

These avenues include:

Diversify Your Earnings: Sponsorship For More YouTube Revenue

Sponsorships are a great way to generate revenue from YouTube once your views, engagement, and subscriber list is at a healthy level.

To use sponsorship, you can collaborate with other brands, channels, and great businesses within your niche, and then use mentions and video plugs to drive traffic and sales to specific product pages and using affiliate marketing, earn a commission of the sale price every time one of your valued followers uses your link to buy something you have recommended.

Still in relation to sponsorship, once you have a healthy following, build a community around your niche topic, and establish your authority and trust-ability within your niche, you can approach businesses you would like to partner with (or promote their product), and for a fee, allow them access to your audience.

Video logs (Vlogs) especially those in a series/playlist-like manner, are especially effective ways to generate YouTube passive income from sponsorships. You can infuse all forms of sponsorship (even affiliate marketing) into your video content through product reveals and show-offs. This approach is especially effective in the fashion niche (or any niche primary concentrated in products) where you buy products and reveal them as you talk about the products or demonstrate how they are helping make your life better (showing off products). In both cases, you tell viewers the value the product adds to your life and to theirs if they buy, so that when you seamlessly place a sponsored link to the product on your video content (Your YouTube video description area is a great place to do this), users can click and head over to buy the product. When they buy the product, you earn money from the sponsor.

You can also earn money from sponsorship by including product mention in the pre-roll, mid-roll, and end-roll segments of your YouTube content; these types of sponsorships are especially common and effective because they capitalize on visuals.

You can also generate tons of income from creating products reviews. Here, you can choose to create how to use video tutorials on products you use or of interest to your target audience and then integrate links to the product page (or ask the company to sponsor the video). By integrating links within the product video and the video description, you can easily compel your audience to take action that earns you commissions in revenue.

There are tons of ways to leverage your growing YouTube channel to generate revenue. For instance, once your channel shows sustainable growth over time or blows up and goes viral thus helping you create a sustainable business brand, you can choose to sell branded merchandise such as T-shirts, mugs, canvas bags, or any other forms of merchandise on Amazon Merch or using the various online shopping channels.

Moreover, once you have a ready audience, you can also monetize your YouTube viewership by creating digital products such as eBooks, video course or tutorials. As long as you are providing value and users are appreciating this value—which therefore means your channel is growing and you are consistently creating new content—you will never lack ways to monetize your YouTube viewership.

Creating value is more important than monetization because in the end, how much value you create will determine your status within your niche, which shall in effect determine how much your YouTube channel earns.

Before you monetize, therefore, concentrate on providing immense value by providing video content that woos and wows your targeted audience. If you do this really well, the money will surely follow and surpass your expectations. In fact, creating a valuable YouTube channel is how you become a YouTube influencer who generates millions in passive income from YouTube.

Contrary to popular belief, monetizing your YouTube channel is actually the easiest part of the process. Once you provide an audience immense value, they will be more than willing to pay you well for it (this is where you can create your own digital products, collaborate with other brands and business to promote their products and earn affiliate commissions, or even allow advertisers access to your audience through sponsored listings).

Obviously, creating value is but the first step in the process. After producing your valuable video content, you have to edit it to make it of high quality, and then after doing this, upload the video while optimizing it for search so that you can increase your views, subscriptions, shares, and thereby grow your channel.

To learn more about editing your YouTube video, read https://www.entrepreneur.com/article/226771 page.

Moreover, since the niche you pursue will determine how aggressively you can grow your channel—more niche popularity means more demand for valuable niche content—to grow your revenue (and inadvertently, your YouTube channel), encourage your audience to interact with your content. Ask them to comment and share the content they find most helpful on social media and to subscribe to your channel.

You can also grow your audience by adding a blog element to your YouTube business, which we talked about earlier by saying how an effective SEO strategy it is; that is how you create a successful YouTube channel that attracts millions of views and subscribers as well as one that rewards you well by generating an income.

CONCLUSION

If you implement the strategies discussed within this actionable YouTube success manual, there is no doubt in my mind that you will create a great and successful channel that pays you well.

Like most things, remember that growing a YouTube channel is a time and resource intensive endeavor. Pace yourself, and if you are relatively new to the prospect, give yourself ample time for growth. Remember that as you get started and go about implementing the numerous lessons outlined in each section, your skills as a YouTube creator will improve impressively, and the easier it will be to make your channel valuable and a capable cash-generating business.

We have come to the end of the book. Thank you for reading and congratulations on reading until the end.

If you found the book valuable, can you recommend it to others? One way to do that is to post a review on Amazon.

Thank you and good luck!

www.ingramcontent.com/pod-product-compliance
Lightning Source LLC
LaVergne TN
LVHW051748050326
832903LV00029B/2794

* 9 7 8 1 7 1 9 9 4 0 0 0 9 *